HOT CROSS BUNS

Traditional

Moderately

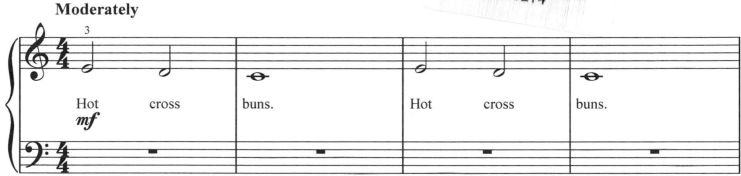

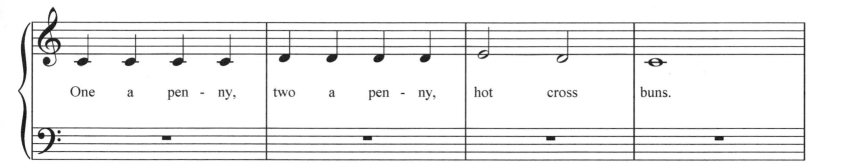

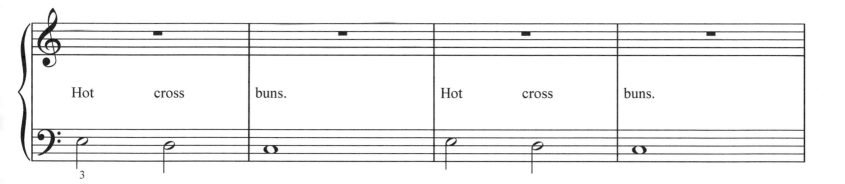

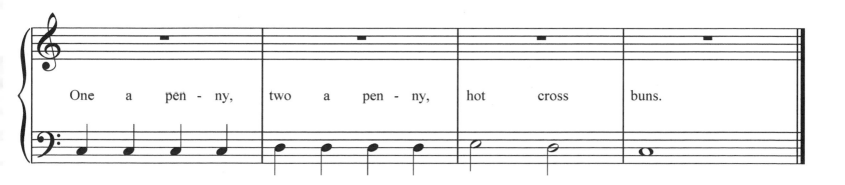

YANKEE DOODLE

Traditional

Energetically

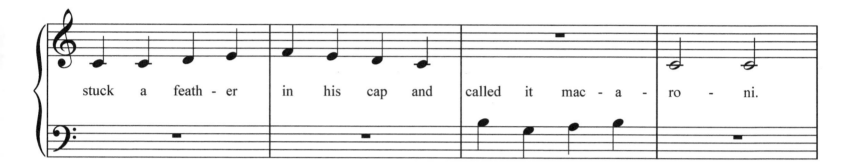

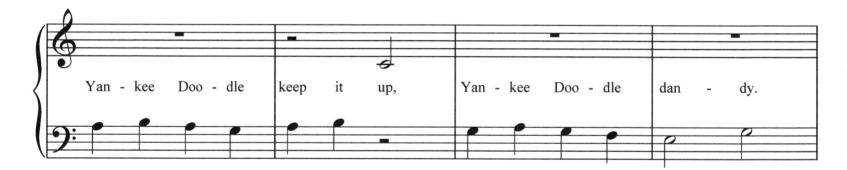

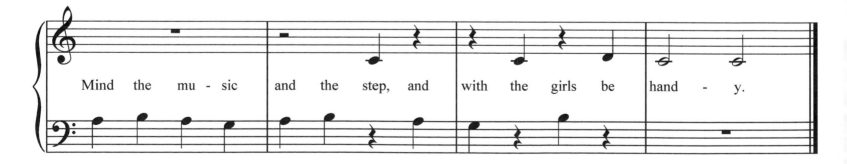

TWINKLE, TWINKLE LITTLE STAR

Traditional

Gently

Twin - kle, twin - kle lit - tle star; how I won - der what you are.

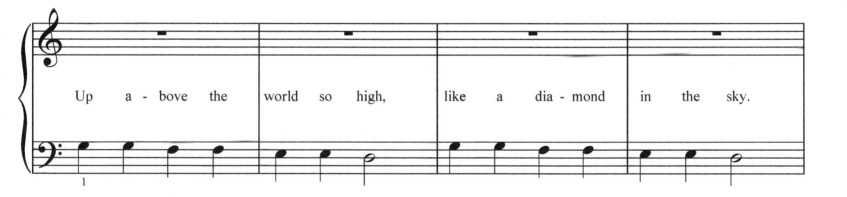

Up a - bove the world so high, like a dia - mond in the sky.

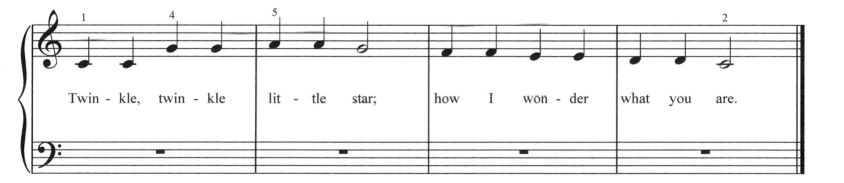

Twin - kle, twin - kle lit - tle star; how I won - der what you are.

LONG, LONG AGO

By THOMAS BAYLY

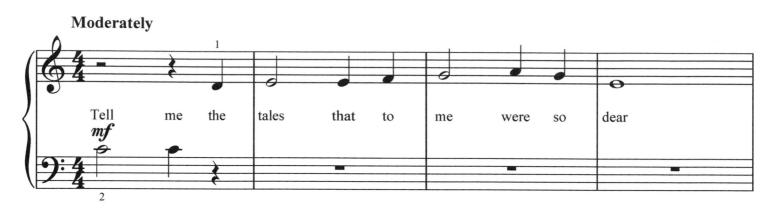

Tell me the tales that to me were so dear

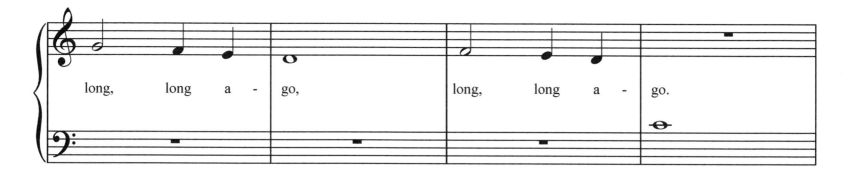

long, long a - go, long, long a - go.

Sing me the song I de - light - ed to hear

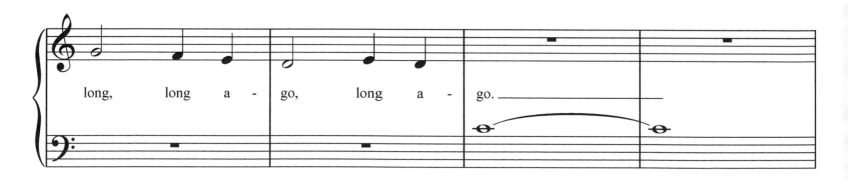

long, long a - go, long a - go.

Now you are come, all my grief is re - moved,

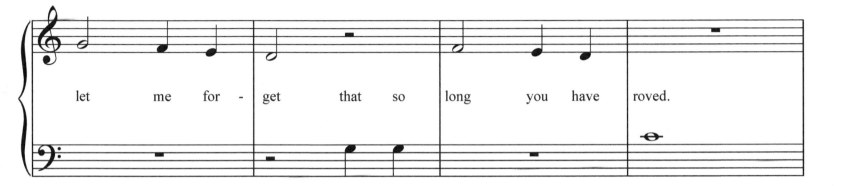

let me for - get that so long you have roved.

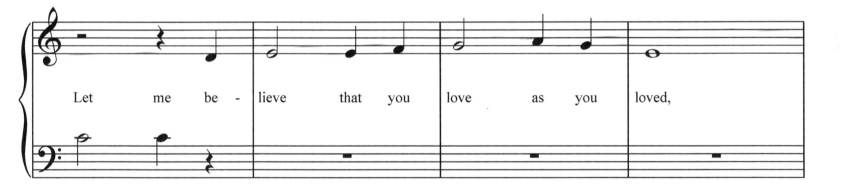

Let me be - lieve that you love as you loved,

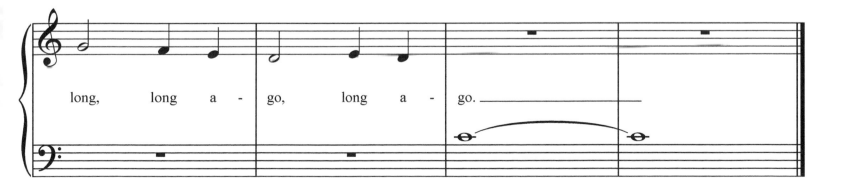

long, long a - go, long a - go.

HAPPY BIRTHDAY TO YOU

Words and Music by MILDRED J. HILL
and PATTY S. HILL

Moderately

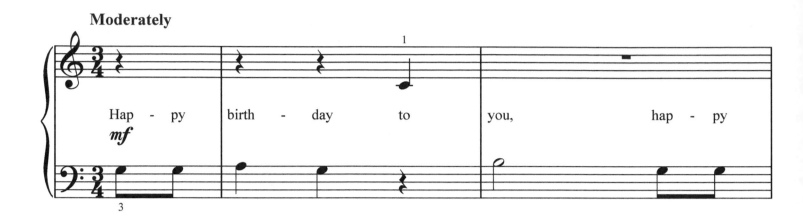

Hap - py birth - day to you, hap - py

birth - day to you. Hap - py birth - day, dear

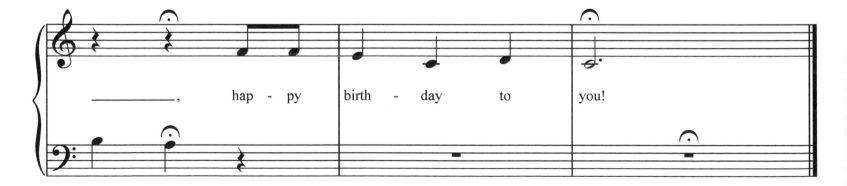

_____, hap - py birth - day to you!

SUPERCALIFRAGILISTICEXPIALIDOCIOUS

from MARY POPPINS

Words and Music by RICHARD M. SHERMAN
and ROBERT B. SHERMAN

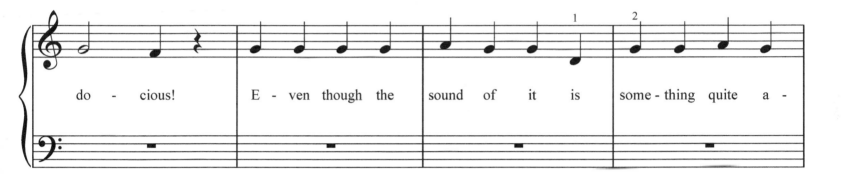

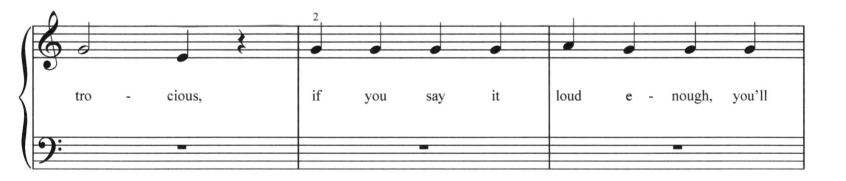

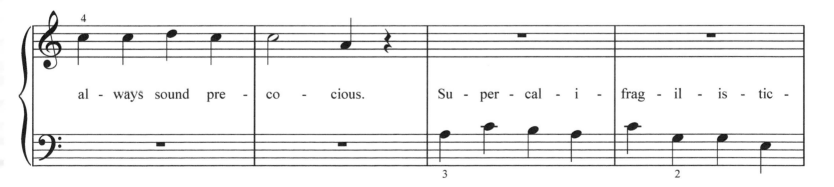

To Coda ⊕

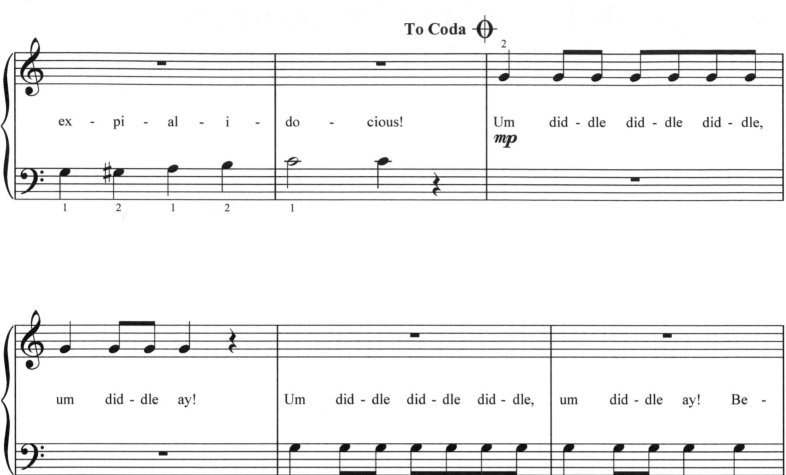

ex - pi - al - i - do - cious! Um did - dle did - dle did - dle,

mp

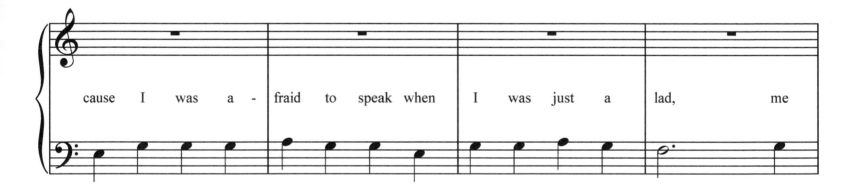

um did - dle ay! Um did - dle did - dle did - dle, um did - dle ay! Be -

cause I was a - fraid to speak when I was just a lad, me

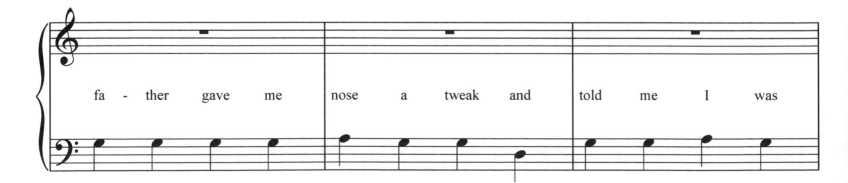

fa - ther gave me nose a tweak and told me I was

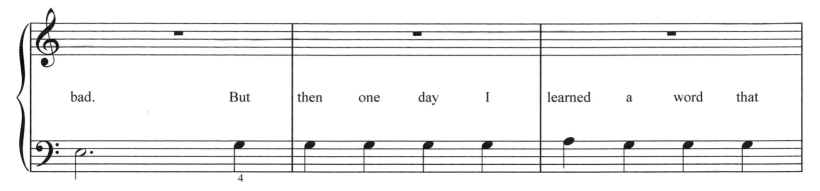

bad.   But   then   one   day   I   learned   a   word   that

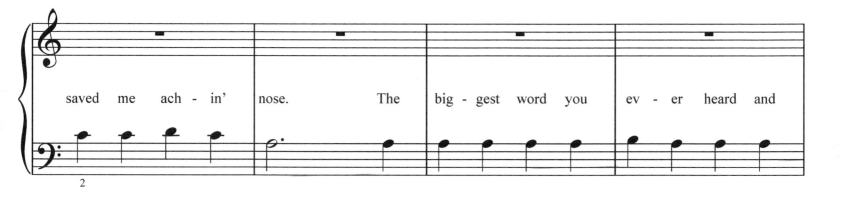

saved   me   ach - in'   nose.   The   big - gest word you   ev - er heard and

D.C. al Coda   **CODA**

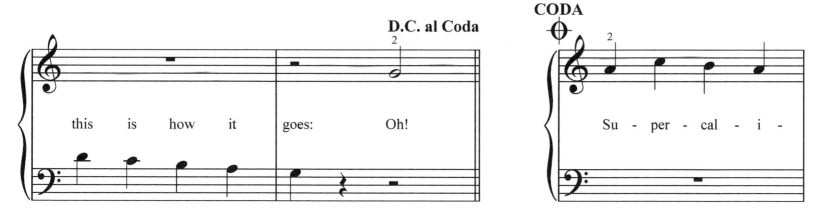

this   is   how   it   goes: Oh!   Su - per - cal - i -

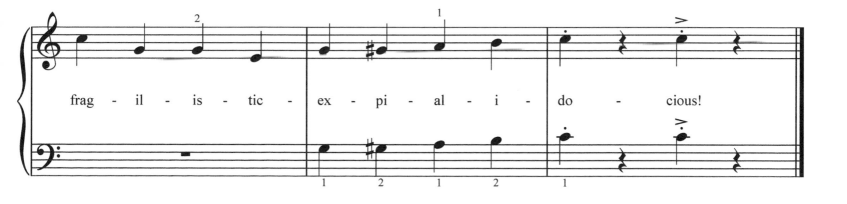

frag - il - is - tic - ex - pi - al - i - do - cious!

CHOPSTICKS

By ARTHUR DE LULLI

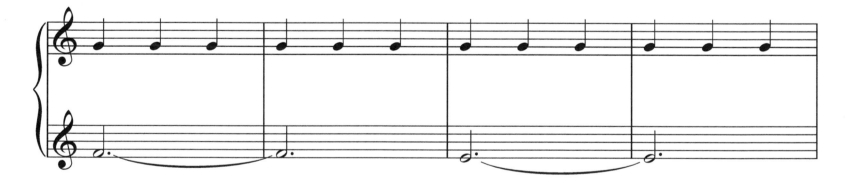

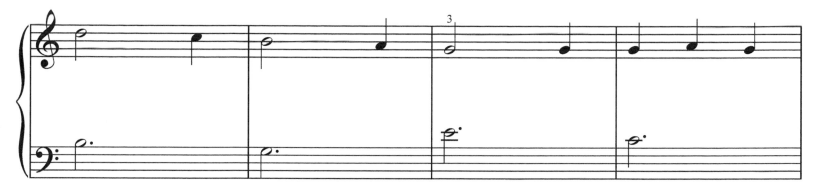

THE CHICKEN DANCE

By TERRY RENDALL
and WERNER THOMAS
English Lyrics by PAUL PARNES

Do you wan-na feel good, wan-na laugh and play? (Let's laugh and play.) Wan-na have some fun, throw your blues a-way? (Your blues a-way.) Are you feel-in'

sad?   Got a prob - lem? Here's a cure. (We got the

To Coda

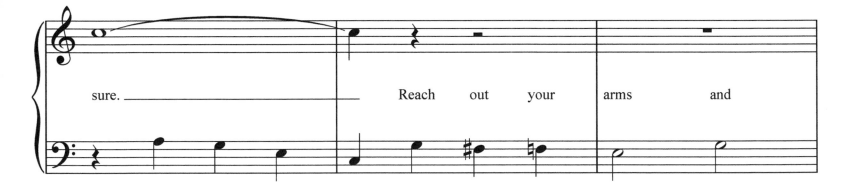

cure.) Do the chick - en dance;   make you hap - py for

sure. _____ Reach out your arms and

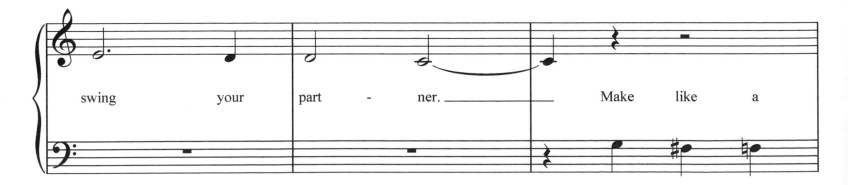

swing your part - ner. _____ Make like a

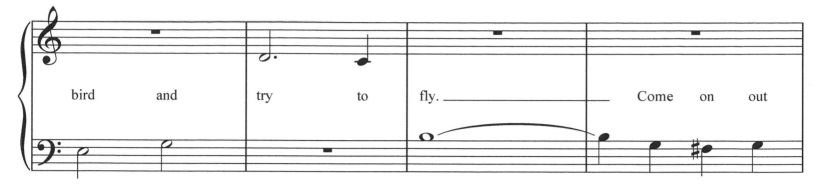

bird   and   try   to   fly. _____   Come   on   out

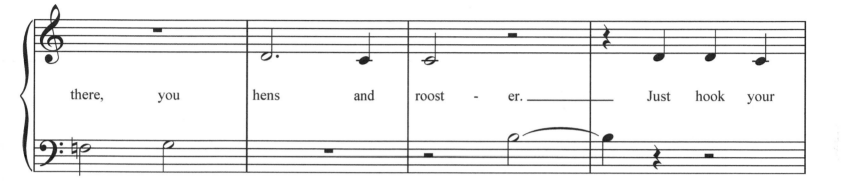

there,   you   hens   and   roost - er. _____   Just   hook   your

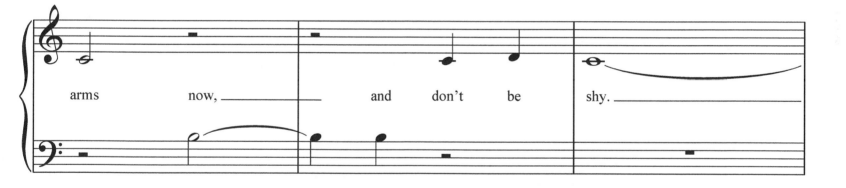

arms   now, _____   and   don't   be   shy. _____

D.S. al Coda

____ Do you wan - na feel

CODA

sure. _____

TAKE ME OUT TO THE BALL GAME

Words by JACK NORWORTH
Music by ALBERT VON TILZER

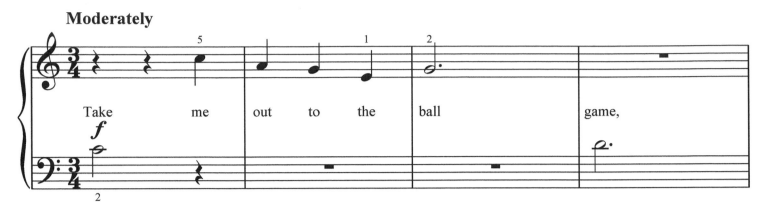

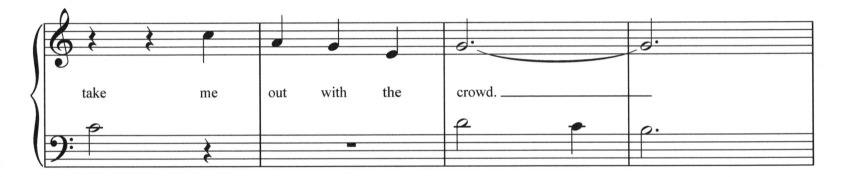

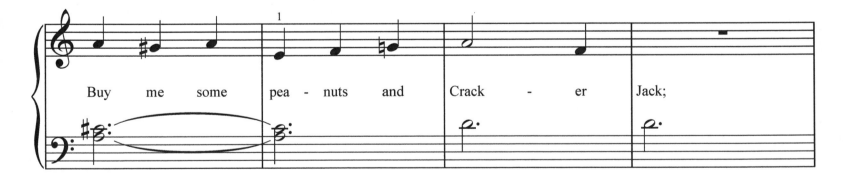

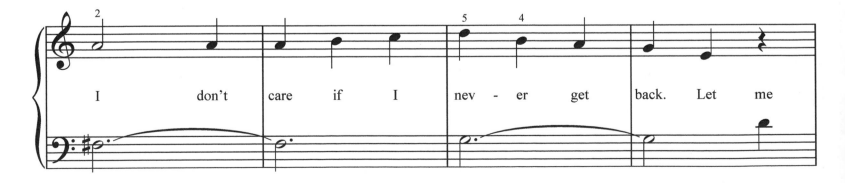

root,　　root,　root　for　the　home　　team,　　if

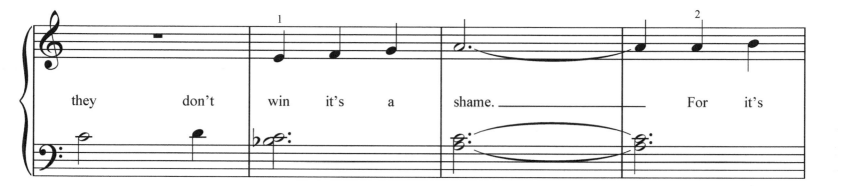

they　　don't　　win　it's　a　shame.＿＿＿＿＿＿＿＿For　it's

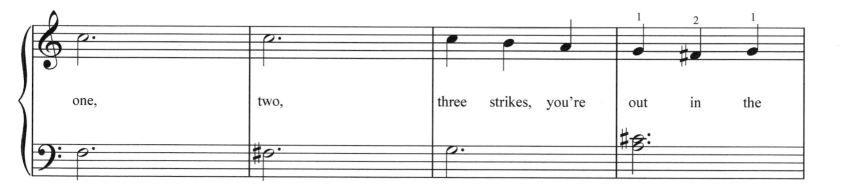

one,　　　two,　　　three　strikes,　you're　out　in　the

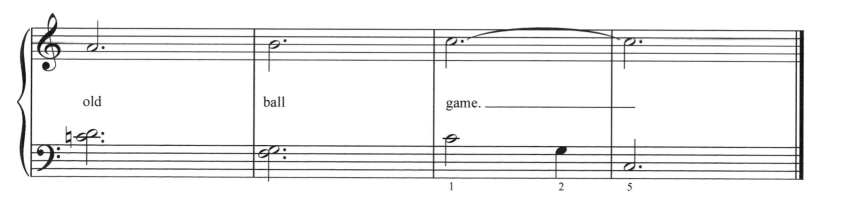

old　　ball　　game.＿＿＿＿＿＿＿＿

DO-RE-MI

from THE SOUND OF MUSIC

Lyrics by OSCAR HAMMERSTEIN II
Music by RICHARD RODGERS

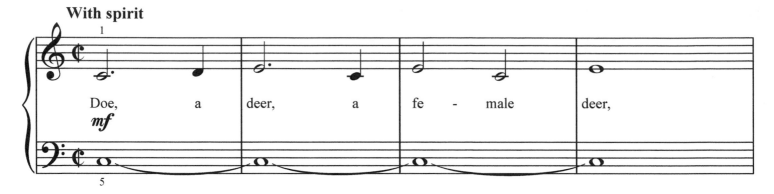

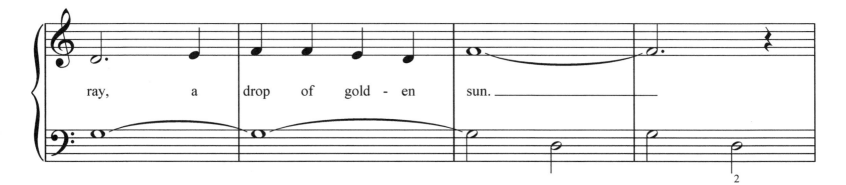

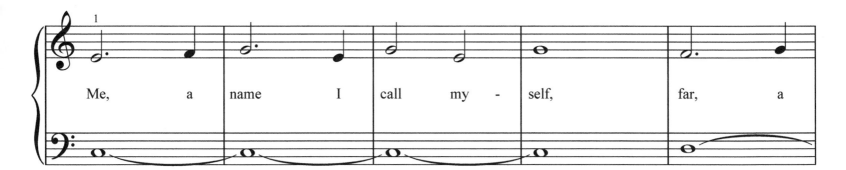

needle pull - ing thread._____ La, a note to fol - low

sew._____ Tea, a drink with jam and bread

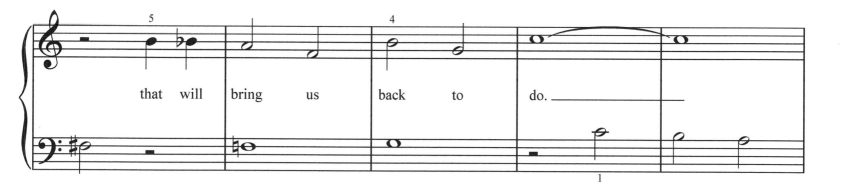

that will bring us back to do._____

Do re me fa sol la ti do._____

YOU ARE MY SUNSHINE

Words and Music by
JIMMIE DAVIS

Moderately

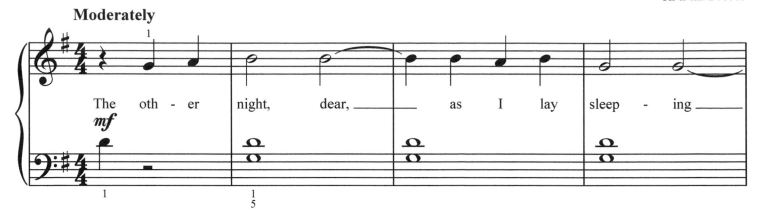

The oth - er night, dear, _____ as I lay sleep - ing _____

mf

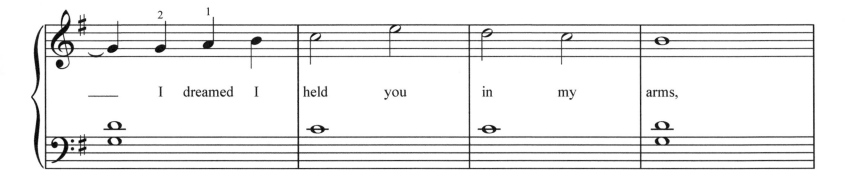

_____ I dreamed I held you in my arms,

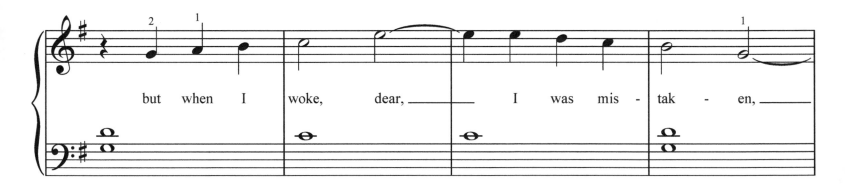

but when I woke, dear, _____ I was mis - tak - en, _____

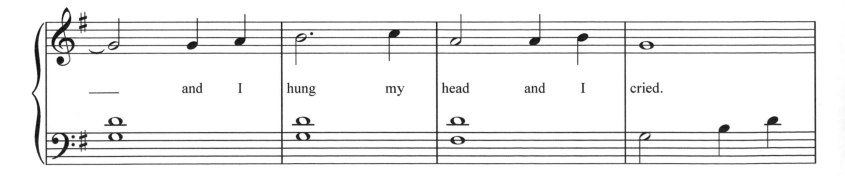

_____ and I hung my head and I cried.

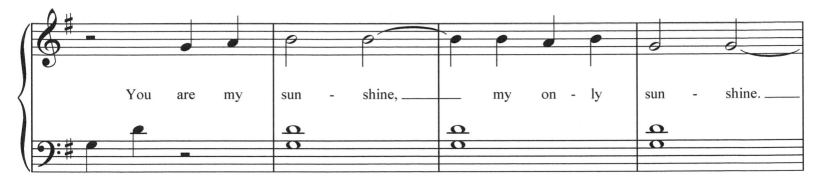

You are my sun - shine, ___ my on - ly sun - shine. ___

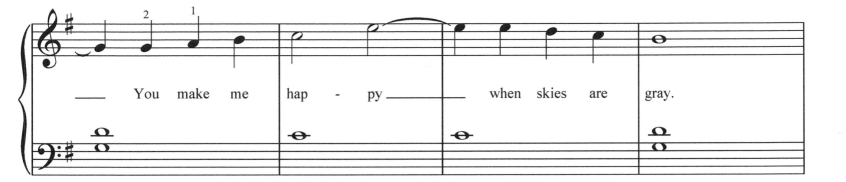

___ You make me hap - py ___ when skies are gray.

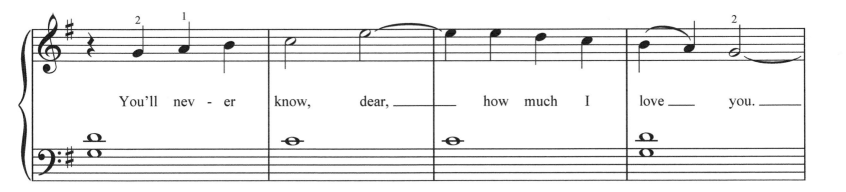

You'll nev - er know, dear, ___ how much I love ___ you.

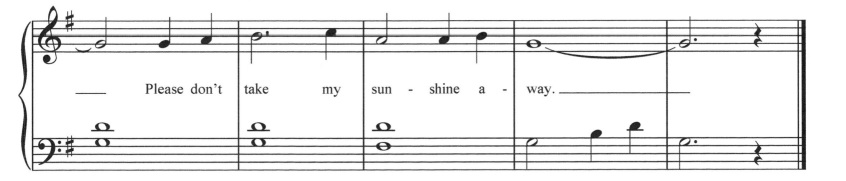

___ Please don't take my sun - shine a - way. ___

CATCH A FALLING STAR

Words and Music by PAUL VANCE
and LEE POCKRISS

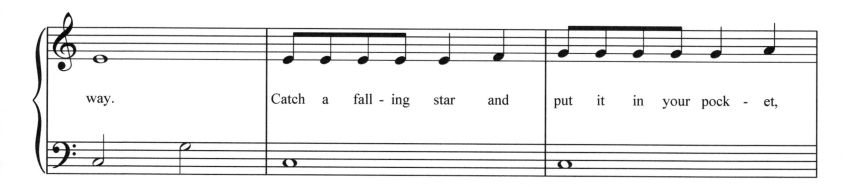

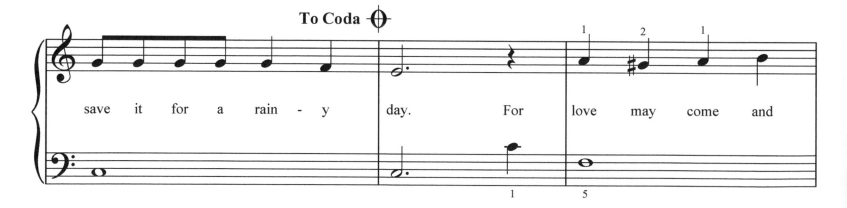

tap you on the shoul - der, some star - less night. And

just in case you feel you want to hold her, you'll have a

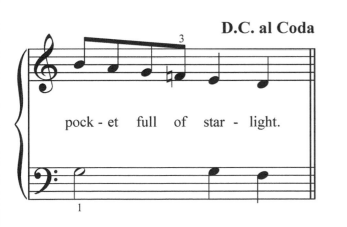

D.C. al Coda

pock - et full of star - light.

CODA

day. Save it for a

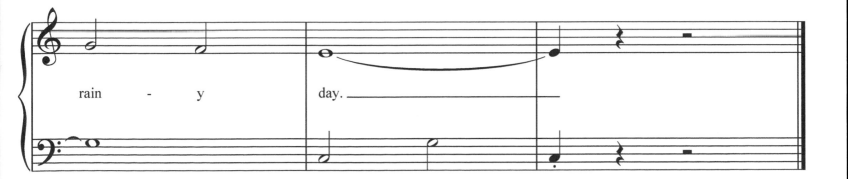

rain - y day.

PUFF THE MAGIC DRAGON

Words and Music by LENNY LIPTON
and PETER YARROW

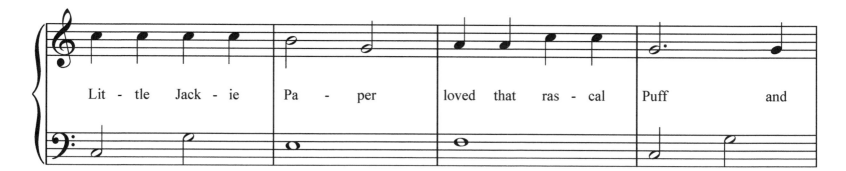

stuff.　　Oh!　　Puff　　the　　mag - ic　　drag - on

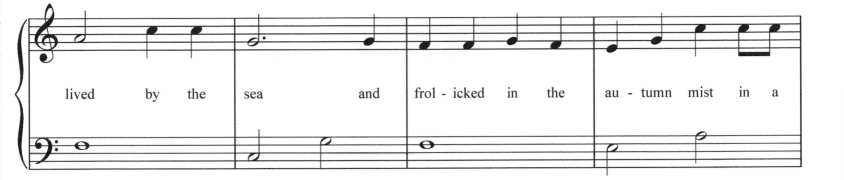

lived　　by　　the　　sea　　　and　　frol - icked　in　　the　　au - tumn mist　in　a

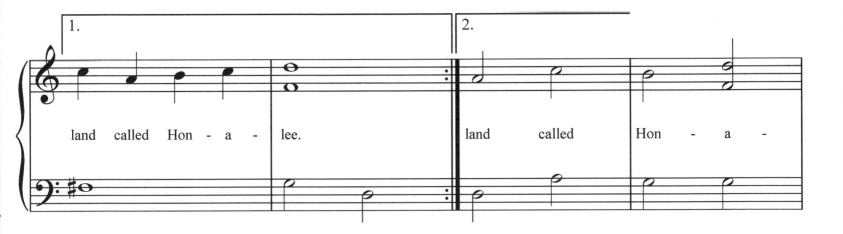

1.　　　　　　　　　　　　　　　　　2.

land　called　Hon - a - lee.　　　　　land　　called　　Hon - a -

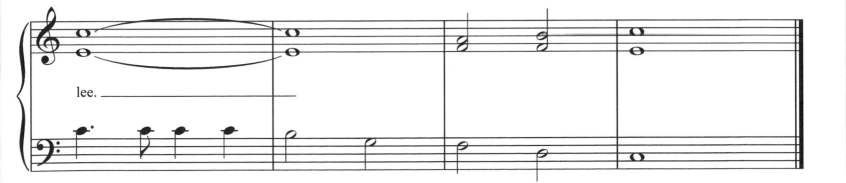

lee. _____

THIS LAND IS YOUR LAND

Words and Music by
WOODY GUTHRIE

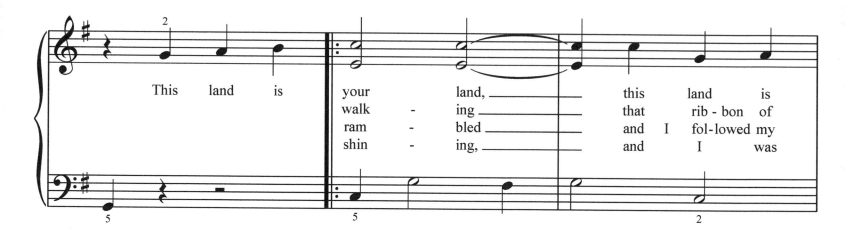

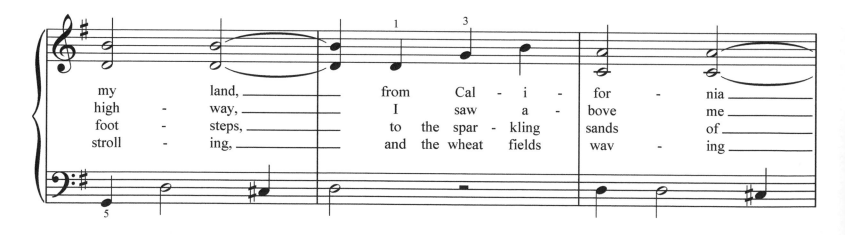

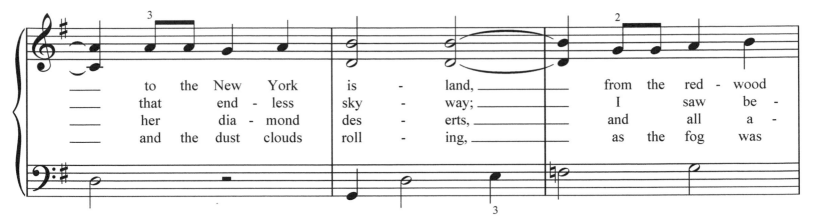

to the New York is - land, _____ from the red - wood
that end - less sky - way; _____ I saw be -
her dia - mond des - erts, _____ and all a -
and the dust clouds roll - ing, _____ as the fog was

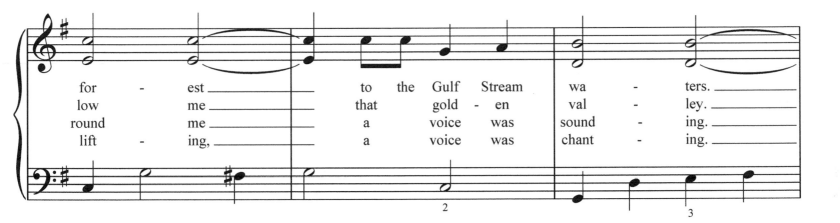

for - est _____ to the Gulf Stream wa - ters. _____
low me _____ that gold - en val - ley. _____
round me _____ a voice was sound - ing. _____
lift - ing, _____ a voice was chant - ing. _____

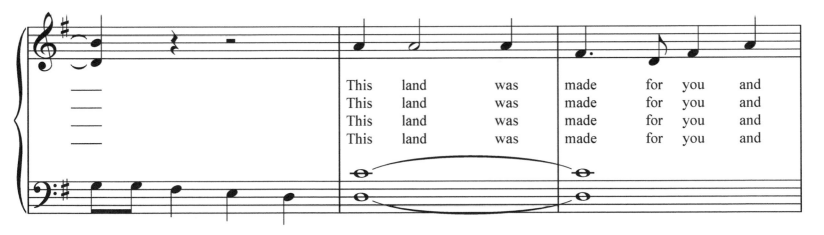

_____
_____ This land was made for you and
_____ This land was made for you and
_____ This land was made for you and
_____ This land was made for you and

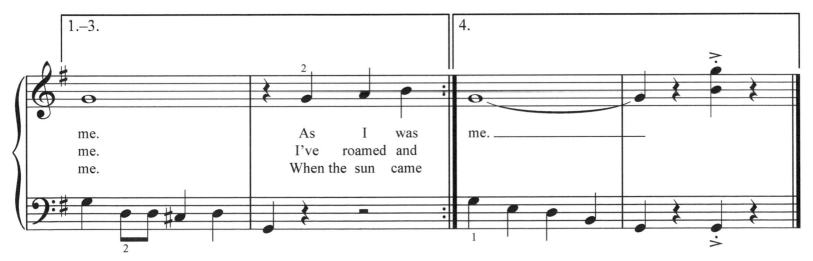

1.–3.   **4.**

me.   As I was   me. _____
me.   I've roamed and
me.   When the sun came

TOMORROW
from the Musical Production ANNIE

Lyric by MARTIN CHARNIN
Music by CHARLES STROUSE

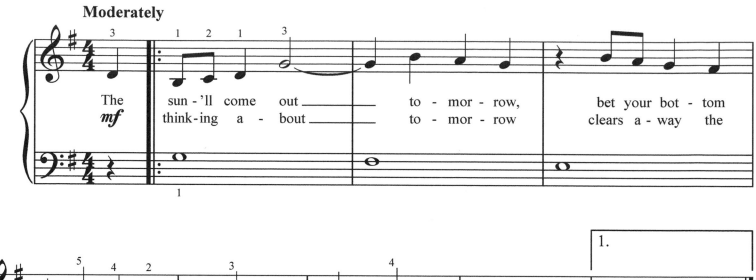

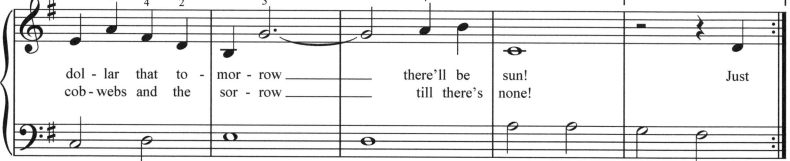

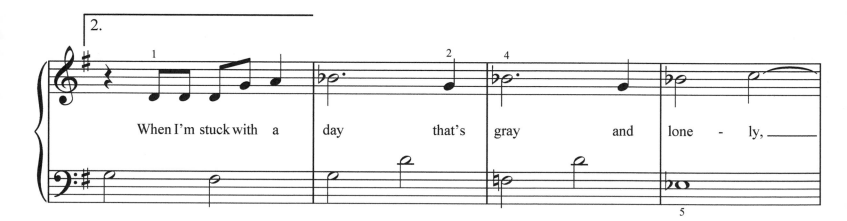

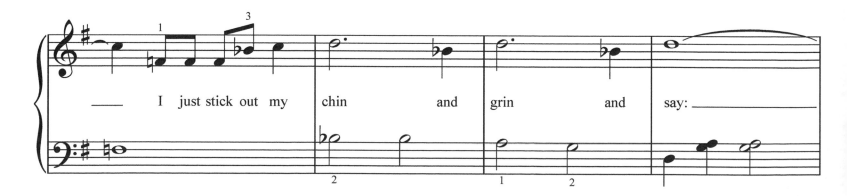

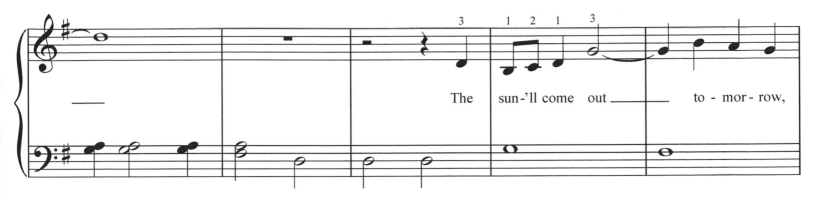

The sun-'ll come out _____ to - mor - row,

so you got to hang on till to - mor - row, _____ come what

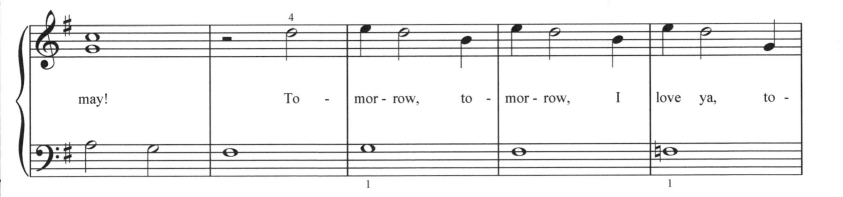

may! To - mor - row, to - mor - row, I love ya, to -

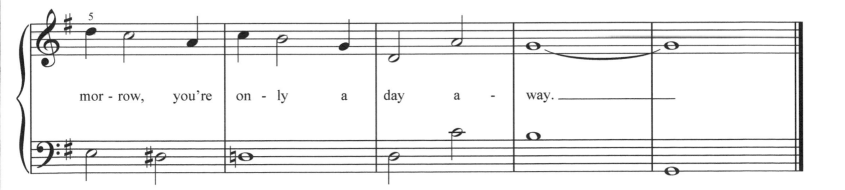

mor - row, you're on - ly a day a - way. _____

SOMEWHERE OUT THERE

from AN AMERICAN TAIL

Music by BARRY MANN
and JAMES HORNER
Lyric by CYNTHIA WEIL

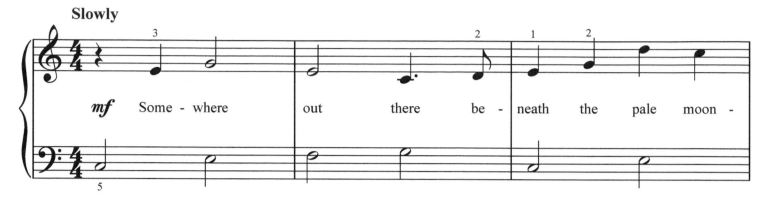

Slowly

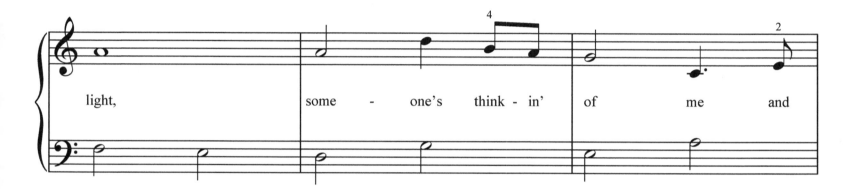

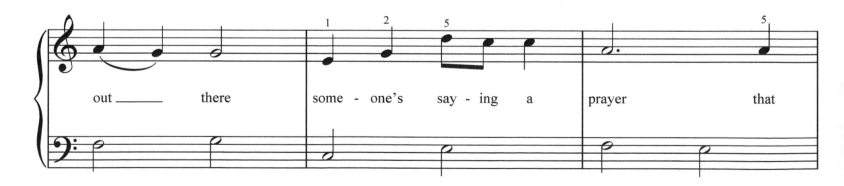

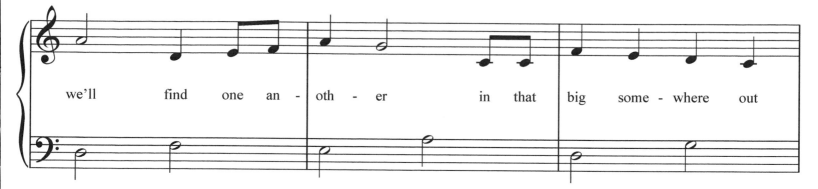

we'll find one an - oth - er in that big some - where out

there. And e - ven though I know how ver - y far a - part we are, it

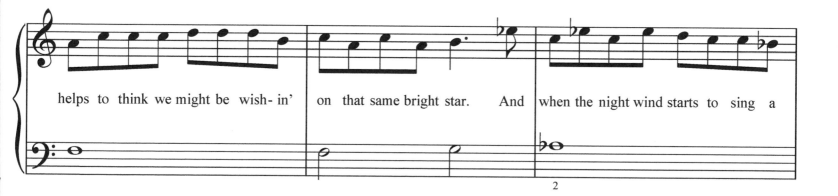

helps to think we might be wish- in' on that same bright star. And when the night wind starts to sing a

lone - some lul - la - by, it helps to think we're sleep - ing un - der -

33

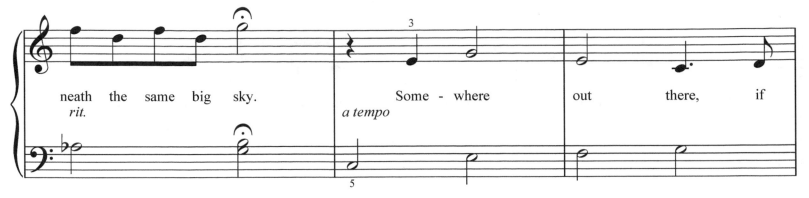

neath the same big sky.
rit.   *a tempo*
Some - where out there, if

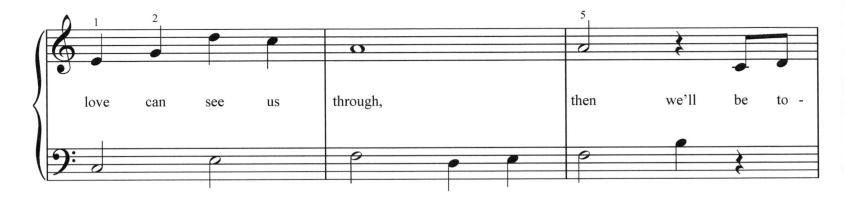

love can see us through, then we'll be to -

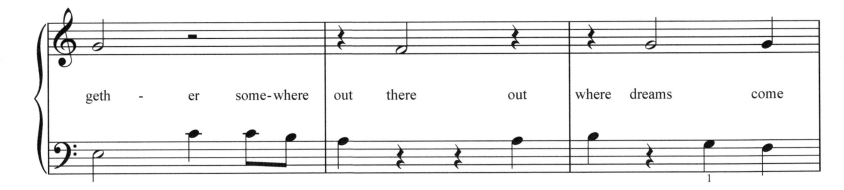

geth - er some-where out there out where dreams come

true. _____   *rit.*

POP GOES THE WEASEL

Traditional

Moderately

All a-round the cob - bler's bench, the mon-key chased the wea - sel. The

mon - key thought 'twas all ___ in fun. Pop, goes the wea - sel. A

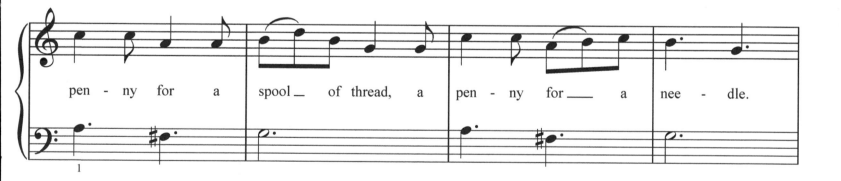

pen - ny for a spool ___ of thread, a pen - ny for ___ a nee - dle.

That's the way the mon - ey goes. Pop, goes the wea - sel.

ROW, ROW, ROW YOUR BOAT

Traditional

Brightly

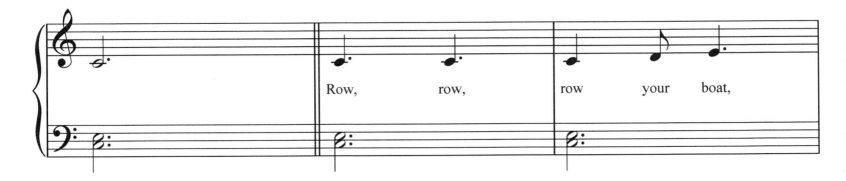

Row,   row,   row your   boat,

gen - tly down the   stream.   Mer - ri - ly, mer - ri - ly,

mer - ri - ly, mer - ri - ly.   Life   is   but   a   dream.

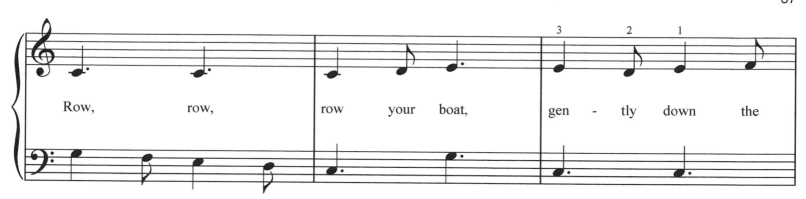

Row, row, row your boat, gen - tly down the

stream. Mer - ri - ly, mer - ri - ly,

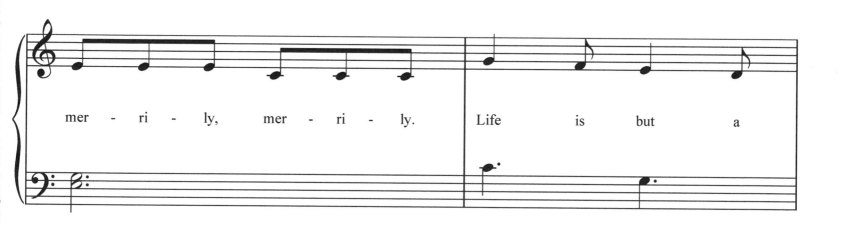

mer - ri - ly, mer - ri - ly. Life is but a

dream.

IF YOU'RE HAPPY AND YOU KNOW IT

Words and Music by
L. SMITH

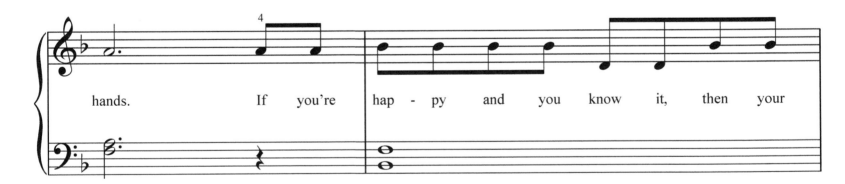

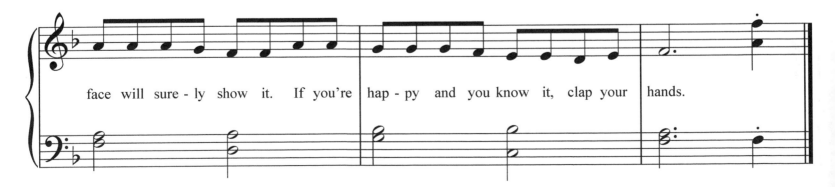

THE HOKEY POKEY

Words and Music by CHARLES P. MACAK,
TAFFT BAKER and LARRY LaPRISE

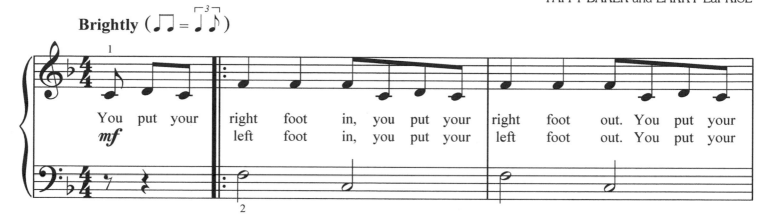

STAR WARS
(Main Theme)
from STAR WARS: A NEW HOPE

Music by JOHN WILLIAMS

Majestically

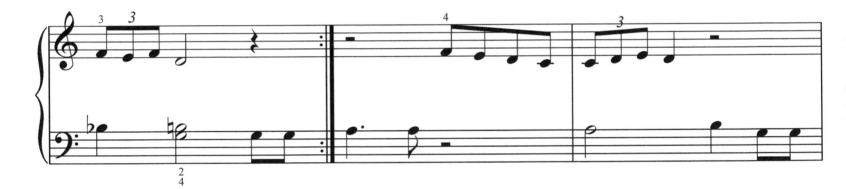

SING
from SESAME STREET

Words and Music by
JOE RAPOSO

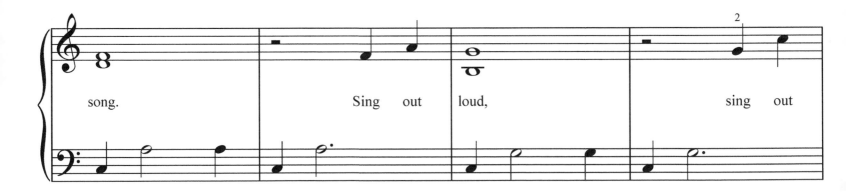

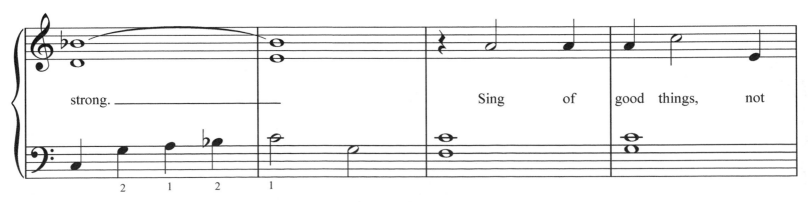

bad.   Sing   of   hap - py   not

sad.   Sing!   Sing   a

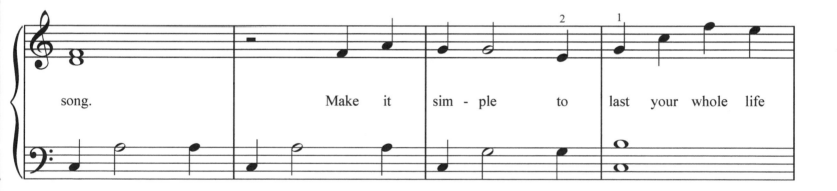

song.   Make   it   sim - ple   to   last   your   whole   life

long.   Don't   wor - ry   that   it's   not

44

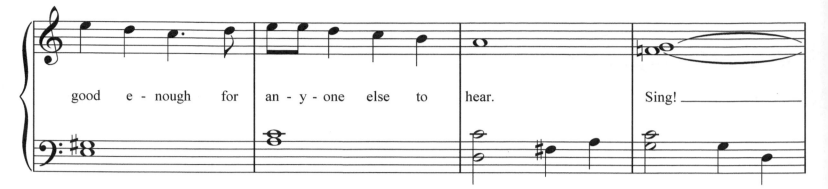

good e - nough for an - y - one else to hear. Sing! _____

_____ Sing a song. La la do la da, la

da la do la da, la da da la do la da. La la do la da, la

da la do la da, la da da la do la da.

A WHOLE NEW WORLD

from ALADDIN

Music by ALAN MENKEN
Lyrics by TIM RICE

Moderately

world,

shin - ing, shim - mer - ing, splen - did.

Tell me, prin - cess, now when did you last let your heart de -

cide? I can o - pen your eyes,

46

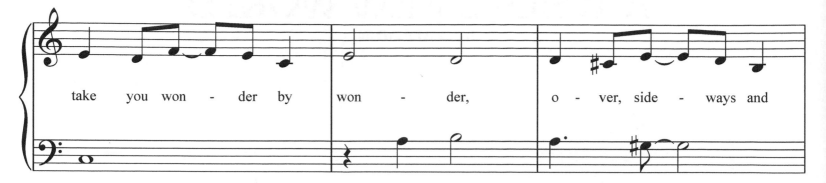

take you won - der by won - der, o - ver, side - ways and

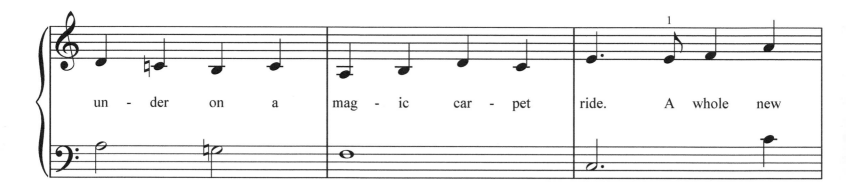

un - der on a mag - ic car - pet ride. A whole new

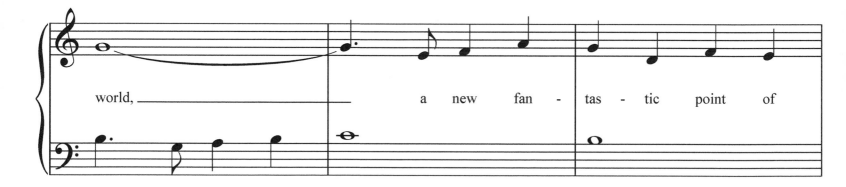

world, _____ a new fan - tas - tic point of

view. No one to tell us no, or where to go or

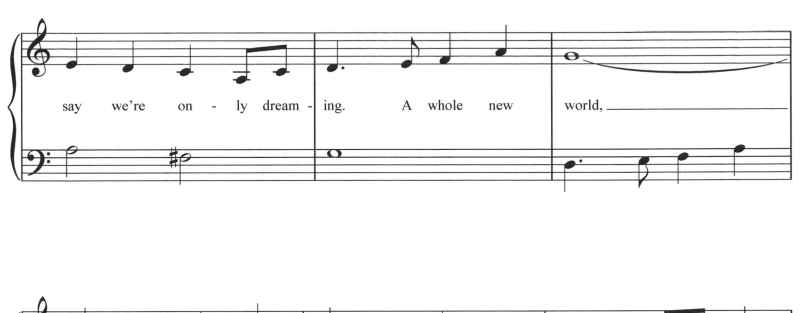

say we're on - ly dream - ing. A whole new world, _____

_____ a daz - zling place I nev - er knew. But when I'm

way up here it's cry - stal clear, that now I'm in a

whole new world with you.

OCTOPUS'S GARDEN

Words and Music by
RICHARD STARKEY

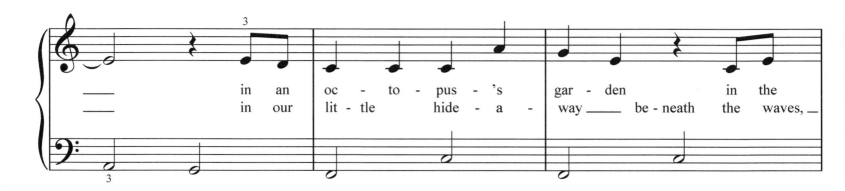

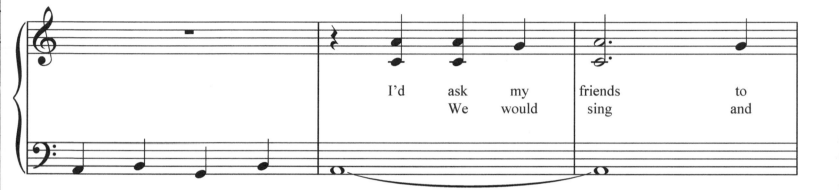

50

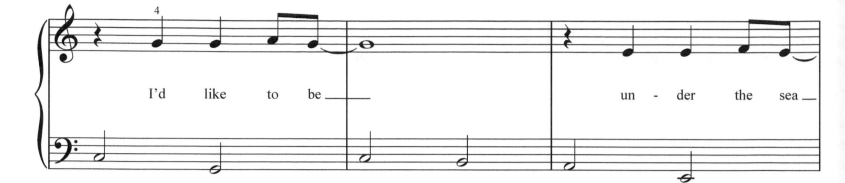

I'd like to be ____ un - der the sea ____

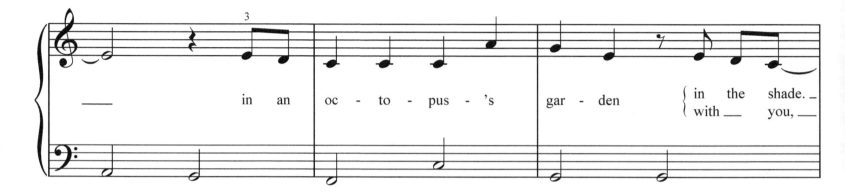

____ in an oc - to - pus - 's gar - den { in the shade. ____ / with ____ you, ____

1. | 2.

____ in an oc - to - pus - 's

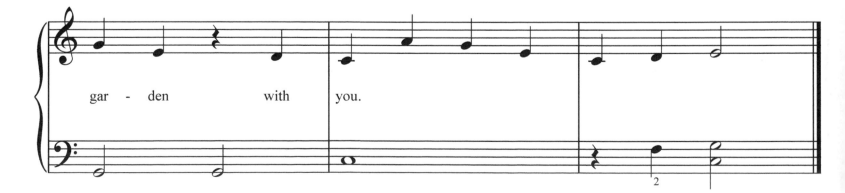

gar - den with you.

LET IT GO
from FROZEN

Music and Lyrics by KRISTEN ANDERSON-LOPEZ
and ROBERT LOPEZ

Half-time feel

The snow glows white on the moun-tain to - night, _ not a foot-print ____ to be seen. _

A king-dom of i - so - la - tion, and it

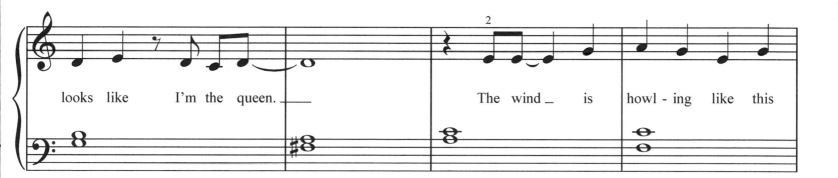

looks like I'm the queen. ____ The wind _ is howl-ing like this

swirl - ing storm in - side. _____ Could - n't keep it in, _

heav-en knows I ____ tried. Don't let ____ them

in, don't let them see, be the good girl you al - ways have to

be. Con - ceal, don't feel, don't let them know... Well, now _

____ they know. ____ Let it go, ____ let it go, ____ can't _

hold it back an - y - more. ____ Let it go, ____ let it go, _

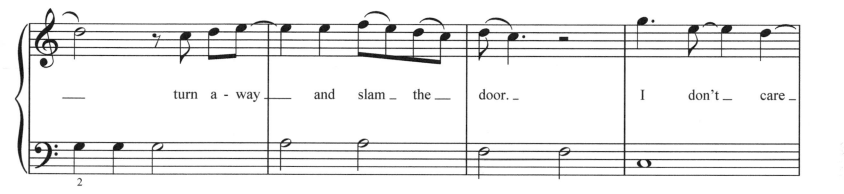

_ turn a - way ____ and slam _ the _ door. _ I don't _ care _

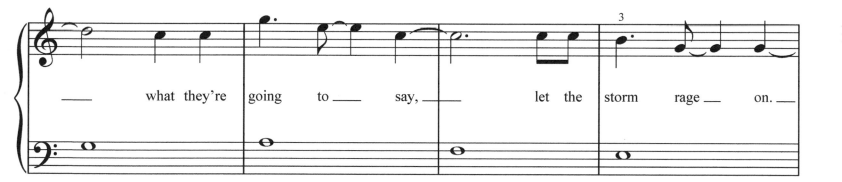

____ what they're going to ____ say, ____ let the storm rage ____ on. ____

____ The cold nev - er both-ered me an - y - way. ____

CAN YOU FEEL THE LOVE TONIGHT

from THE LION KING

Music by ELTON JOHN
Lyrics by TIM RICE

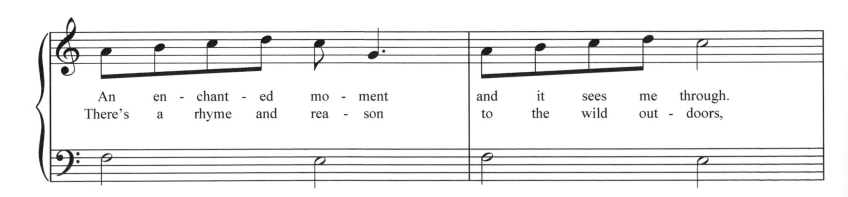

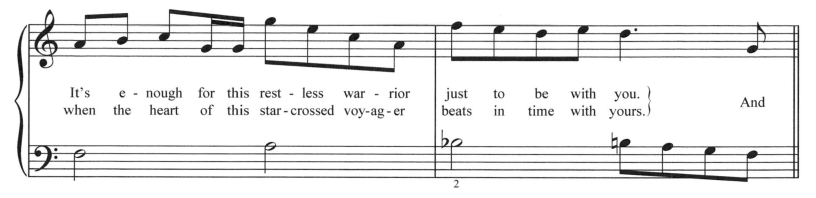

It's   e - nough for this rest - less war - rior   just   to   be   with   you.
when   the   heart   of this star - crossed voy-ag - er   beats   in   time   with yours.

And

2

can   you   feel   the   love   to - night? _____
can   you   feel   the   love   to - night? _____

It   is   where   we   are.   It's   e - nough   for this
How it's   laid   to   rest?   It's   e - nough   to make

2

wide - eyed   wan - der - er   that   we   got   this   far.   And
kings   and   va - ga - bonds be -

56

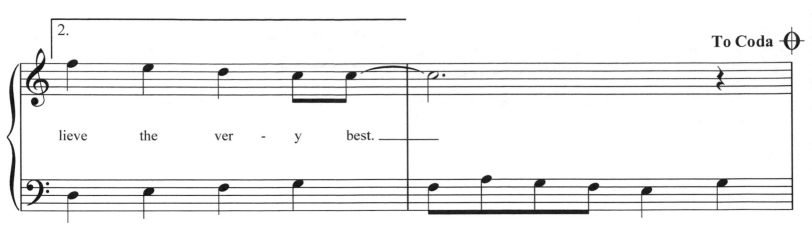

To Coda

D.S. al Coda
(take repeat)

CODA

It's e - nough to make

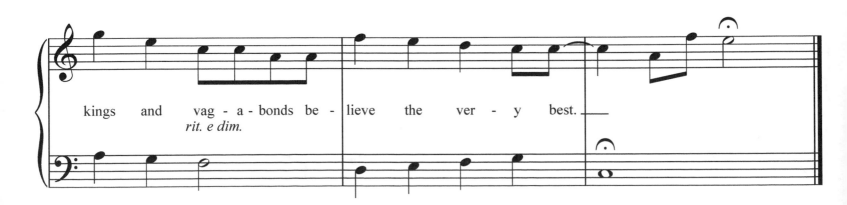

kings and vag - a - bonds be - lieve the ver - y best.
rit. e dim.

THREE LITTLE BIRDS

Words and Music by
BOB MARLEY

Moderately slow Reggae

Don't

wor - ry   a - bout a   thing,   'cause

ev - 'ry lit - tle thing   gon - na be al - right.   Sing - in', don't

58

worry a - bout a thing, 'cause

ev - 'ry lit - tle thing gon - na be al - right. Rise up this

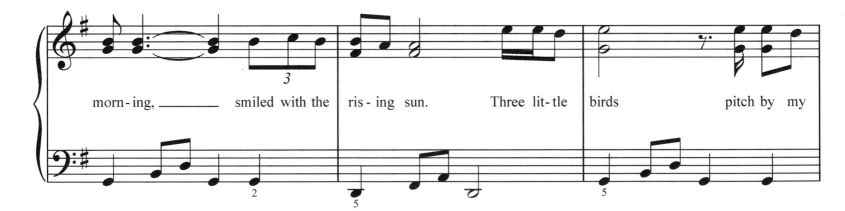

morn - ing, _____ smiled with the ris - ing sun. Three lit - tle birds pitch by my

door - step, _____ sing - in' sweet songs of mel - o - dies pure and true, say - in',

"This is my mes-sage to you- oo - oo." _____ Sing-in', don't | oo - oo." _____ Sing-in', don't

wor - ry   a - bout a   thing,   'cause ev -'ry lit - tle thing   gon - na be al -

right.   Sing - in', don't wor - ry   a - bout a   thing,   'cause

ev -'ry lit - tle thing   gon - na be al - right.

BEST DAY OF MY LIFE

Words and Music by ZACHARY BARNETT,
JAMES ADAM SHELLEY, MATTHEW SANCHEZ,
DAVID RUBLIN, SHEP GOODMAN
and AARON ACCETTA

Woo, woo, _____

woo.   I   had a dream so big and loud, ___ I
                             howled _ at the moon with friends _ and

jumped so high, I touched the clouds. _____   Whoa, oh oh oh oh oh. _____
then the sun came crash - ing in. _____   Whoa, oh oh oh oh oh. _____

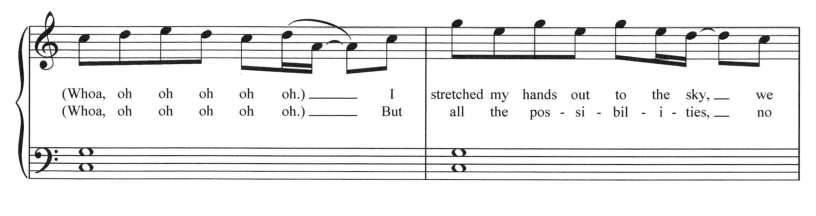

Woo, woo, _____ woo. This is gon - na be the best day of my

life, _____ my life. _____ Woo, woo, _____

woo. This is gon - na be the best day of my life, _____ my

life. _____ Woo, woo, _____

D.S. al Coda

woo. Woo, woo, _____ woo. I

CODA

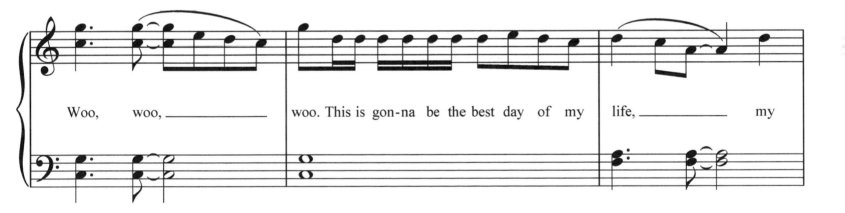

Woo, woo, _____ woo, _____ woo. _____

Woo, woo, _____ woo. This is gon-na be the best day of my life, _____ my

life. _____ Woo, woo, _____ woo. This is gon-na be the best day of my

life, _____ my | life. _____ | Woo, woo. _____

Ev-'ry-thing is look-ing up, ev-'ry-bod-y up now. | Woo, woo. _____

This is gon-na be the best day of my | life. _____

This is gon-na be the best day of my | life. _____